DINOSAUR WORLDS

DINOSAURS
RULERS OF THE EARTH

DON LESSEM

David Wright,
28th February 1999

Heinemann

DINOSAUR WORLDS: DINOSAURS – RULERS OF THE EARTH
was produced by Bender Richardson White, Uxbridge, UK.

Editors: Lionel Bender, Andy Boyles
Designer: Ben White
Editorial Assistants: John Stidworthy, Madeleine Samuel
Media Conversion and Typesetting:
Peter MacDonald and Diacritic
Production: Kim Richardson
Senior Scientific Consultant: Dr Peter Dodson, Professor of Anatomy and Geology at the University of Pennsylvania School of Veterinary Medicine, and Vice-President of the Dinosaur Society.

First published in the USA in 1996 by
Highlights for Children, Honesdale, Pennsylvania 18431.

This edition published in Great Britain in 1996 by Heinemann Children's Reference, an imprint of Heinemann Educational Publishers, a division of Reed Educational and Professional Publishing Limited, Halley Court, Jordan Hill, Oxford OX2 8EJ.

MADRID ATHENS
FLORENCE PRAGUE WARSAW
PORTSMOUTH NH CHICAGO SAO PAULO MEXICO
SINGAPORE TOKYO MELBOURNE AUCKLAND
IBADAN GABORONE JOHANNESBURG KAMPALA NAIROBI

ISBN 0 431 05660 9 Hb ISBN 0 431 05664 1 Pb

British Library Cataloguing-in-Publication Data.
A catalogue record for this book is available from the British Library.

Printed in Spain

This book is recommended by the Dinosaur Society UK. For more information please contact The Dinosaur Society UK, P O Box 329, Canterbury, Kent, CT4 5GB

Acknowledgements
Photographs Pages: 5 and 10: Dr Paul Sereno. 13: Norbert Wu/Natural History Photo Agency. 14 –15: Oxford Scientific Films/C.C. Lockwood, Earth Scenes. 16, 17: Dr Paul Sereno. 20: Francois Gohier Pictures. 24–25: George W. Frame. 26: Francois Gohier Pictures. 30: The Natural History Museum, London. 33: Oxford Scientific Films/London Scientific Films. 34–35: Natural History Photo Agency/A. N. T. 36 and 37 (all photos): The Natural History Museum, London. 40: Earthwatch, Massachusetts. 44: Lory Herbison Frame. 46: Bill Hopkins/Dr P. Vickers-Rich, Monash Science Centre, Monash University. 47: Dr P. Vickers-Rich.
Illustrations All major double-page scenes by Steve Kirk. All other major illustrations by James Field. Ecology diagrams and small featured creatures by Jim Robins. Step-by-step sequences by John James. Maps by Ron Hayward. Cover illustration by Steve Kirk.

GLOSSARY

The Cretaceous Period lasted from 145 million to 65 million years ago. In the Early Cretaceous, 145 million to 97 million years ago, vertebrates included not only the dinosaurs featured in this book, but also the following:

Amphibians Animals that lay eggs in water but usually spend most of their adult lives on land. Modern amphibians include newts and frogs.
Ichthyosaurs (ICK-thee-o-saws) Fish-shaped, air-breathing marine reptiles that ate fish. They lived throughout the Cretaceous Period.
Labyrinthodonts (LAB-uh-RIN-tho-donts) Small flat-bodied amphibians of many forms and sizes, most of which had a pattern like a maze (or labyrinth) inside their teeth.
Lungfish Fish that have lungs as well as gills and so can breathe air. They can survive droughts or live in stagnant waters.
Mammals (MAM-uls) Animals with hair that nurse their young. Mammals were present throughout the age of dinosaurs, although during that time they never grew larger than domestic cats.
Pterodactyls (TAIR-o-DACK-tills) Pterosaurs with long necks and short tails that grew both small and large in the Jurassic and Cretaceous Periods.
Pterosaurs (TAIR-o-SAWS) Flying reptiles, the first backboned animals to fly.
Reptiles Animals that reproduce by laying hard-shelled or leathery eggs on land. Snakes, lizards, turtles and crocodiles are some of the modern types of reptiles.
Sauropods (SAW-ro-pods) Long-necked, lizard-hipped, plant-eating dinosaurs that walked on all fours.

ECOLOGICAL TERMS
atmosphere the layer of gases that surrounds the Earth; also known as the air.
carnivore a meat-eating animal.
climate the average weather conditions in a particular part of the world.
continent a huge area of land on Earth, such as North America, South America, Europe and Australia.
environment the total living conditions, including landscape, climate, plants and animals.
evolved changed, over many generations, to produce a new species, body feature or way of life.
geography the study of the land, sea and air on Earth.
geology the study of the materials of the Earth's rocks, minerals and fossils and the processes by which they are formed.
habitat the local area in which an animal or plant lives, for example, a desert, forest or lake.
herbivore a plant-eating animal.
migrate to move from place to place as conditions change or to reproduce.
predator a meat-eating animal that hunts and kills.
prey an animal that is hunted and eaten by a predator.
scavenger a meat-eating animal that does not kill its own prey but eats the bodies of animals already dead.
species a group of living things in which individuals look alike and can reproduce with one another.
vegetation plant life.

ABOUT THIS BOOK

Welcome to *Dinosaur Worlds.* In these pages you will see dinosaurs as you have never seen them before – with their fellow animals and plants in the environments they inhabited. Dinosaurs were a highly successful and varied group of land reptiles with fully upright postures and S-curved necks that lived from 228 million to 65 million years ago.

Dinosaurs – Rulers of the Earth explores the environments of the Early Cretaceous Period, which lasted from 145 to 97 million years ago. During the Early Cretaceous, the Earth's two continents began to divide into the seven we know today. New forms of plant-eaters evolved to cope with the changing conditions, and the first flowering plants appeared. This book reveals these worlds as today's leading scientists and artists see them, based on fossil evidence. Fossils are the remains of once-living creatures that have been preserved in the rocks. Comparisons with living animals and habitats help to fill in details that fossils cannot provide.

This book is divided into four chapters, each looking at a specific dinosaur fossil site and revealing a different feature of dinosaur life and death. A short introductory section provides background information about the world at this time.

Enjoy your journey of discovery to the lost worlds of the dinosaurs!

"Dino" Don Lessem

Measurements

This book uses metric units of measure:
centimetre (cm) , metre (m),
kilogram (kilo) and tonne
1cm = 0.4 inches, 1m = 40 inches = 3.3 feet
1 kilo = 2.2 pounds
1 tonne (1,000 kilos) is approximately 1 ton

CONTENTS

Within each chapter of the book are five double-page spreads. The first spread is a large, dramatic scene at the site millions of years ago. The second spread, 'A Look Back In Time', identifies and describes the major animals and plants in the scene and highlights the environment. The next spread, 'Featured Creatures', gives basic facts and figures about the most interesting animals and plants. Spread four, 'Then And Now', compares dinosaurs and their worlds with present-day animals and habitats. The last spread in each chapter, 'How Do We Know?', looks at the scientific evidence for all this – the fossils and what they reveal about the behaviour and ecology of dinosaurs.

THE EARLY CRETACEOUS

During the Early Cretaceous, from 145 million to 97 million years ago, lands separated, creating isolated populations of animals that evolved in different ways. Many new dinosaurs evolved, including efficient plant-eaters and deadly meat-eaters. Climates varied greatly, from the cool darkness of polar lands to the humid tropical swamps. Most plants were similar to those from earlier times, but among them were also the first flowering plants – weedy little herbs. Snakes evolved from lizards. Fish, birds and tiny mammals became more varied.

FOSSIL FINDS AROUND THE WORLD
This map shows the present-day continents and the dinosaur fossil sites from the Early Cretaceous Period. The four sites featured in this book are shown as red dots.

North Africa was close to the equator. All year round it was a hot and swampy region.

Utah 125 million years ago was mostly arid plain, with life concentrated in rivers and nearby forests. New dinosaurs have been discovered here recently, including armoured types and *Utahraptor*, a vicious meat-eater (see page 22).

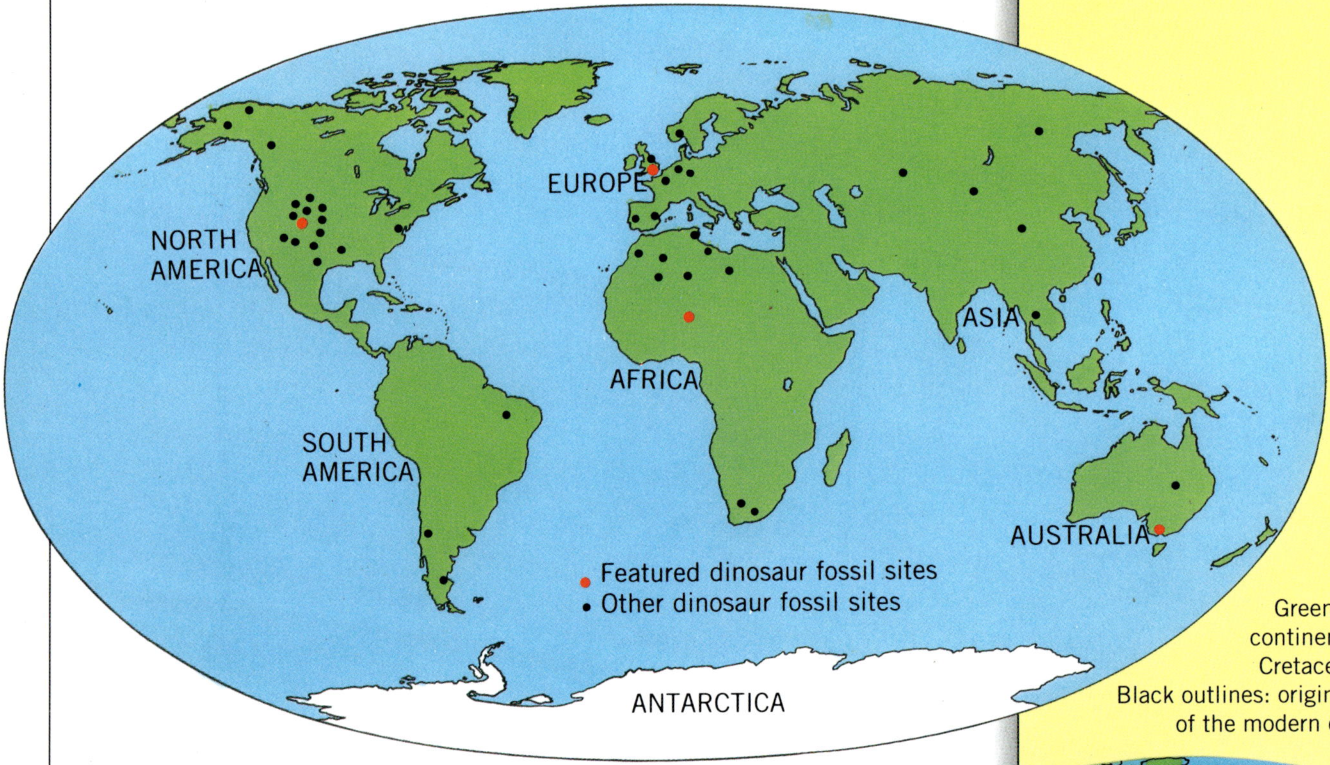

Australia was further south and part of it was within the Antarctic Circle. Some dinosaurs might have lived there through months of winter darkness.

Early Cretaceous **England** was a lowland of forest and marshes. Its dinosaurs included a big fish-eater called *Baryonyx*, and *Iguanodon*, a big herbivore.

CLIMATE

The movement of the great landmasses created a variety of climates during the Early Cretaceous. Inland, the temperatures showed some seasonal variation, and the climate was drier.

CONTINENTS
The continents of the Early Cretaceous – Laurasia in the north and Gondwana in the south – were separated by a shallow widening sea. In the south, Australia, Antarctica and South America were breaking away from one another. India was still close to the west coast of Africa.

Below:
Green areas: the continents in Early Cretaceous times.
Black outlines: original position of the modern continents.

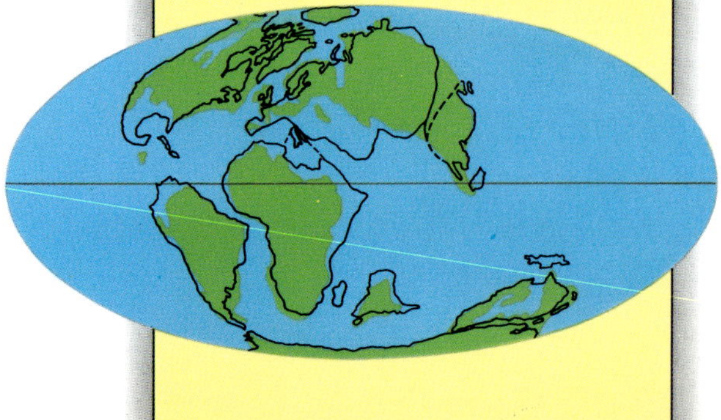

Fossil finds worldwide show that during the Early Cretaceous dinosaurs became smaller on average and developed more advanced types of teeth and claws. In North America, the giant four-legged plant-eaters called sauropods had died out, but similar forms still lived in North Africa and elsewhere. Other giant plant-eaters survived in South America, and still others lived on in Asia. A new type of large plant-eater with teeth adapted for grinding plants appeared and succeeded worldwide. These dinosaurs, the iguanodontids, may have been well-suited for eating the new plants that were appearing – flowering herbs.

Other new dinosaurs were savage hunters, including giant large-clawed predators (see pages 20–27). Armoured dinosaurs and small bird-hipped dinosaurs also became more common in the Early Cretaceous Period (see pages 40–47).

Palaeontologist Dr Paul Sereno cleans rock debris from the fossilized upper-arm bone of a large plant-eating dinosaur in the Sahara Desert in Niger, North Africa. He and his crew of scientists from the University of Chicago in the US discovered the dinosaur on an expedition in 1987. In that year and on a return journey in 1993, Dr Sereno's team found the remains of species of both large plant-eating dinosaurs and meat-eaters (see pages 16–17).

A NEW HERBIVORE: *Iguanodon*

Of all the different types of dinosaurs in the Early Cretaceous Period, *Iguanodon* and its close relatives were the most successful and widespread, and left the most fossils. Using fossils and other evidence, scientists and artists try to recreate *Iguanodon*'s life. They hope to understand how it interacted with the plants and other animals in its environment.

Bones do not hold the answers to every question about an animal's diet, posture, body temperature, skin or internal organs. But scientists can make reasonable guesses about these details by comparing extinct creatures with living animals. In addition, some basic ideas about biology – such as how animals kept a constant body temperature – seem to hold true for many different kinds of creatures. Here we show how some of this knowledge is applied to the iguanodontid group of plant-eaters.

GEOLOGICAL TIME
Dinosaurs lived during the Mesozoic Era, from 245 million to 65 million years ago. The Cretaceous Period, 145 million to 65 million years ago, was the final period of the Mesozoic.

HIPS
Iguanodon was a **bird-hipped**, or ornithischian, dinosaur – the pubis bone of its hips pointed backwards and down, alongside the ischium bone. In **lizard-hipped** dinosaurs, or saurischians, the pubis pointed forwards and the ischium bone backwards.

SPINE AND TAIL
Across the vertebrae that made up *Iguanodon*'s backbone and tailbones, bony tendons overlapped, strengthening the spine and helping to hold up the tail.

COLD-BLOODED LIFESTYLE
Reptiles are cold-blooded, which means they rely on surrounding temperatures to warm their bodies. They bask in the sun **(1, 2)** to increase their body heat, then shelter beneath rocks or vegetation **(3)** to retain warmth as the air cools at night. Also, they often change the angle of their bodies towards the sun to adjust their rate of warming **(4, 5)**. Meat-eating dinosaurs are believed to be the ancestors of birds. Birds today are warm-blooded. But new studies of the bones of birds from dinosaur times show that early birds were not yet fully warm-blooded. This suggests that many dinosaurs may have been cold-blooded.

In the Late Cretaceous, descendants of the iguanodontids, the duck-billed dinosaurs, were among the most common plant-eaters. Some scientists have suggested that the success of these plant-chewers was linked to the spread of flowering plants in the Cretaceous Period. Perhaps these herbivores were better able to feed upon the low-growing plants than were their predecessors, the long-necked sauropods.

POSTURE

Iguanodon was built to walk upright on its toes. It had long foot bones and three toes on each foot that were spread out to support the animal's weight of more than 4 tonnes. Fleshy toe pads may have helped cushion *Iguanodon*'s step.

OLD IDEAS

Iguanodon was named in 1825, even before the term *dinosaur* was used (see page 36). It was one of the first dinosaurs found. During the past 170 years, this prehistoric animal has been reconstructed in ways quite unlike our present understanding of its appearance.

The first models of *Iguanodon* showed a four-legged rhinoceros-like creature with its thumb claw misplaced (as a horn) on its snout. Later reconstructions of the skeleton showed the dinosaur posed upright like a kangaroo, with a bent tail resting on the ground – a pose that would have broken *Iguanodon*'s tail.

HEAD

Iguanodon had a sharp toothless beak, perhaps designed to grab and tear off plants. Its cheeks held many leaf-shaped teeth. To chew plants, *Iguanodon* used its teeth in an up-and-down grinding motion.

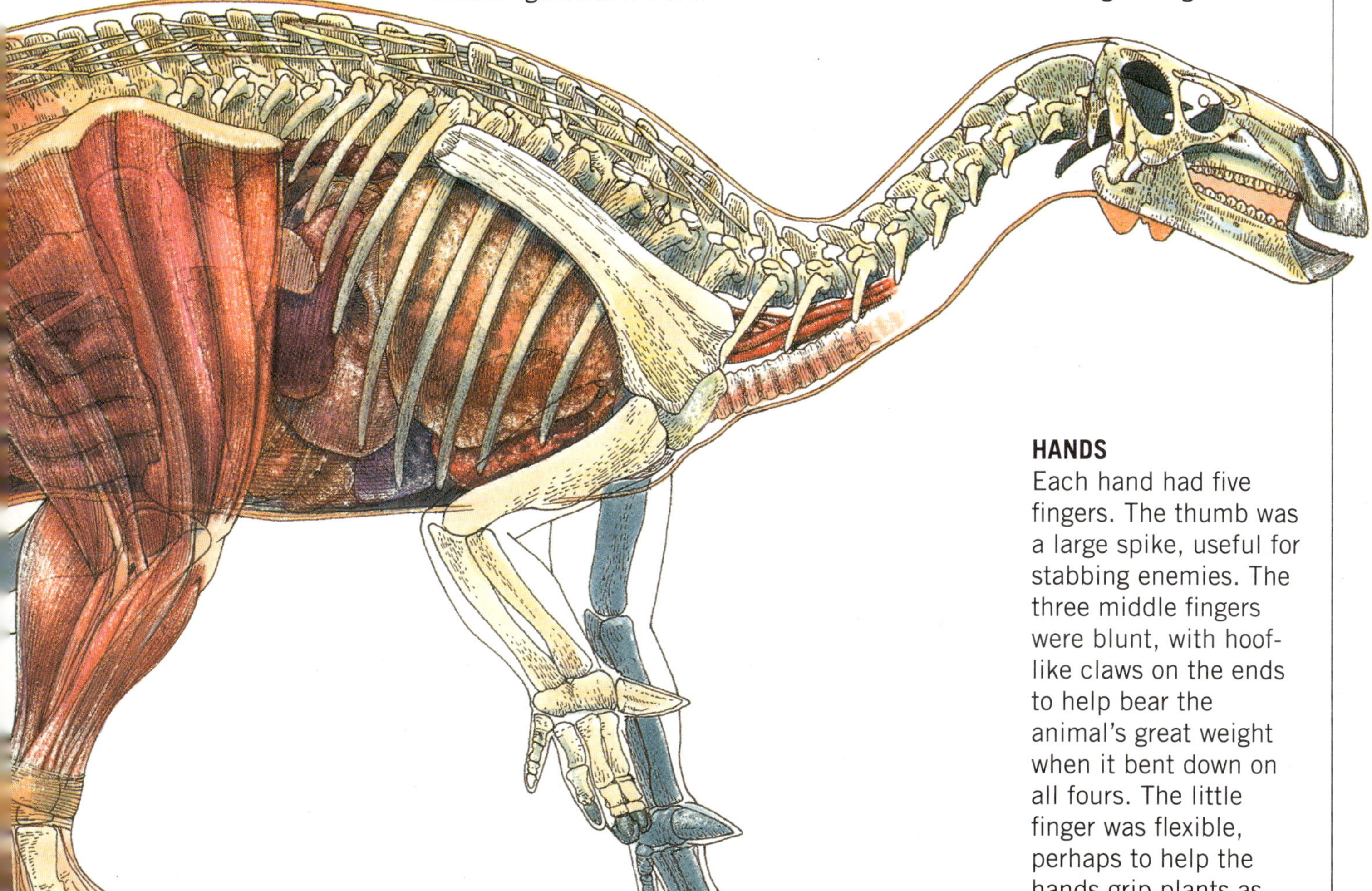

HANDS

Each hand had five fingers. The thumb was a large spike, useful for stabbing enemies. The three middle fingers were blunt, with hoof-like claws on the ends to help bear the animal's great weight when it bent down on all fours. The little finger was flexible, perhaps to help the hands grip plants as the dinosaur ate. (See also pages 32–33.)

AN ANCIENT SWAMPLAND

SAHARA DESERT

Niger, North Africa

130 million years ago

Near the equator, the climate is hot and wet. A 15-metre-long crocodile lurks in a coastal river, and a shark preys on other fish in the warm water. On the riverbank, large predatory dinosaurs close in on a huge plant-eater.

NEW SOUTHERN ANIMALS

In Early Cretaceous North Africa, some very odd-looking new dinosaurs appeared. In this region there was a fascinating mixture of newer dinosaur types living among creatures that resembled giants of an earlier time.

During the Cretaceous Period, each part of the world was beginning to develop its own particular dinosaur community. Throughout most of Gondwana, new kinds of big plant-eaters and meat-eaters became the dominant dinosaurs.

But in North Africa, there were dinosaurs that resembled the big meat-eaters and plant-eaters of Jurassic North America. Examples of these creatures were *Afrovenator*, which is like *Allosaurus*, and a recently discovered sauropod similar to North America's *Camarasaurus*. How did these creatures come to live in North Africa? Perhaps North Africa still had some land linking it to the northern supercontinent, Laurasia, and animals used this land bridge to move between the two areas.

Some of the new North African dinosaurs had sail-fins on their backs, meat-eaters and plant-eaters alike. The sail-backed plant-eaters included a large *Iguanodon*-like bird-hipped dinosaur called *Ouranosaurus*. Scientists think the fins might have worked like radiators to help these dinosaurs lose excess body heat during temperature regulation (see page 6).

Many other new life-forms besides dinosaurs were found in North Africa during the Early Cretaceous Period. They include many early examples of the types of fish and reptiles alive today.

Niger – Today
A convoy of vehicles carrying palaeontologists drives along the edge of the Sahara Desert in Niger. The scientists found tonnes of jumbled dinosaur bones in the remains of a river bottom from 130 million years ago. These Early Cretaceous 'graveyards' held fossils of huge plant-eating dinosaurs and a big carnivorous dinosaur.

By the Early Cretaceous, a group of fish called 'ray-fins' (below) greatly outnumbered all others. Two ray-fins of ancient Niger were *Lepidotes* and a pycnodont. They are called ray-fins because their fins are stiffened by slender, bony rods, or rays. Most modern fish are ray-fins.

Many 'lobe-fins' (which have lobes formed of bone and muscle in their fins) were disappearing. The lungfish *Ceratodus* and the coelacanth *Mawsonia* were lobe-fins of that time. Today, lungfish and coelacanths are the only known survivors of this group.

Also swimming in these waters were 'cartilaginous' fish, which include sharks, rays and other fish with skeletons of cartilage instead of bone. *Hybodus* was an Early Cretaceous shark.

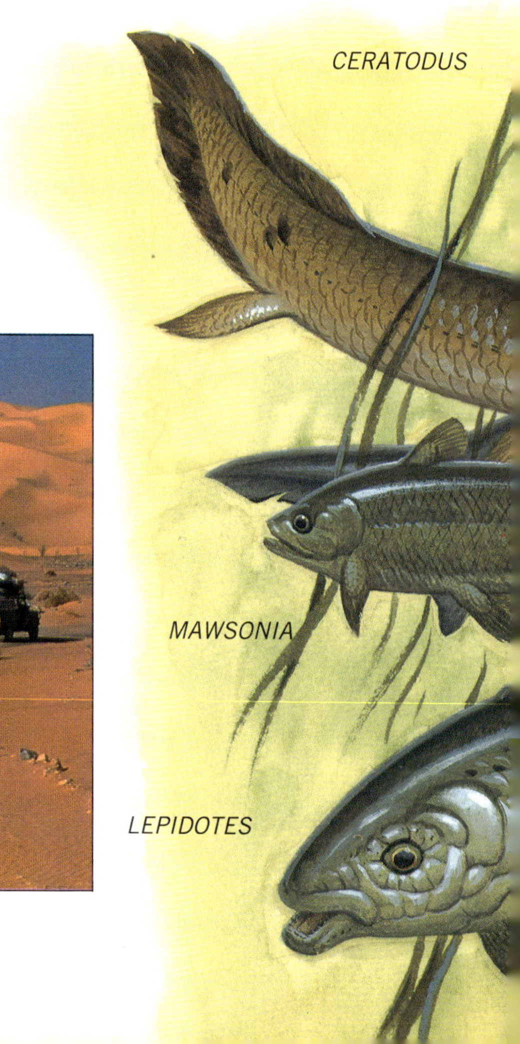

Sahara Desert, Niger – Then
In the hot, wet conditions of 130 million years ago, ferns and ginkgo plants thrive. In these watery lowland forests, the larger trees are *Brachyphyllum* and other conifers. In these woods there is danger. Two *Afrovenator*, 9-metre-long predators, attack their sauropod prey.

Sarcosuchus, longer than any killer dinosaurs from any period, hunts in the river. Two-metre-long *Hybodus* sharks also hunt there. *Trionyx* turtles, 85 centimetres long, feed on plants and insects in the water. The many-finned coelacanth, *Mawsonia,* and the various ray-finned fish are likely victims of the large predators.

FACT FILE

ANIMALS
1. *Afrovenator* (AF-ro-vuh-NAY-tur)
2. *Camarasaurus*-like sauropod (KAM-uh-ruh-SAW-rus)
3. *Hybodus* (hy-BOW-dus)
4. *Lepidotes* (LEH-pih-DOH-tees)
5. *Sarcosuchus* (SAR-ko-SOO-kus)
6. *Trionyx* (try-AW-nicks)

PLANTS
7. *Brachyphyllum* conifer (BRACK-ee-FY-lum)

ALSO AT THIS SITE:
Ceratodus (sair-AH-toe-dus)
Mawsonia
Pycnodonts (PICK-no-dahnts)
Cedar trees
Ferns
Ginkgoes

Niger, Then and Now Today, the place where these Early Cretaceous plants and animals lived is more than 1,600 kilometres north of the equator, and it is mostly desert. As part of Gondwana 130 million years ago, this region was wetter and closer to the equator.

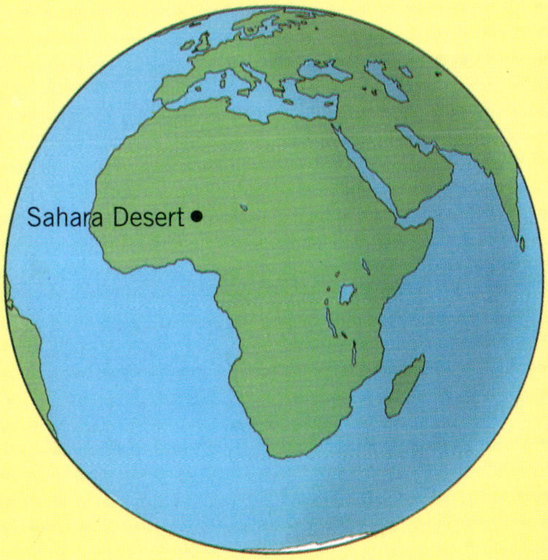

Globe shows the position of the continents now.

SAHARAN SWAMPLANDS

Far from being a desert, the Sahara 130 million years ago was home to fish, turtles, crocodiles and an abundance of plant life. Dinosaurs that had become extinct elsewhere in the world ten million years before – giant four-legged plant-eaters and bulky three-fingered predators – lived on here. Enormous crocodiles dwarfed the dinosaur predators.

Scientists think *Afrovenator* was capable of killing the largest plant-eaters in its world, which were twice its size.

AFROVENATOR

Meaning of name: 'African hunter'
Order: Saurischia
Size, Weight: 9 metres long, 2 tonnes
Location: Niger
Diet: Meat

Afrovenator had a powerful jaw. Its skull, though large, was lightly built, with many holes between the bones. This design reduced the skull's weight without reducing its strength.

Afrovenator was similar to *Allosaurus*, a larger three-fingered predator from western North America in the Late Jurassic. *Afrovenator* was probably a swifter hunter because it was lighter and had longer legs.

The powerful jaws and neck of *Afrovenator* gave added strength to its bite as it snapped and tore at prey.

Afrovenator's strong forelimbs and long curved claws could have been used to seize its victims.

AFROVENATOR

SARCOSUCHUS

Meaning of name: 'Flesh crocodile'
Order: Crocodilia
Size, Weight: 15 metres long, 3 tonnes
Locations: South America, North Africa
Diet: Meat

Sarcosuchus was huge. It might have hunted on land, but its narrow snout suggests it ate mostly fish. Although *Sarcosuchus* was larger than the biggest meat-eating dinosaur, it was not the biggest crocodile ever. *Deinosuchus*, which lived in the American Southwest 65 million years later, was at least as big as *Sarcosuchus*. Long after the dinosaurs, the crocodile *Rhamphosuchus* lived in India. It was probably bigger still, but only its jawbone has been found.

PLANTS

Seed ferns up to 4.5 metres tall were common in swampy forests. Their woody trunks were covered with old leaf bases. The leaves resembled fern fronds and held large seeds. The roots of seed ferns were stilt-like, as are mangrove tree roots in the tropics of today.

Among the conifer trees of Niger 130 million years ago were species similar to the incense cedar of the Pacific coast of North America today. The 'incense' of the tree is a sweet scent in the leaves and wood. South of today's equator is an almost identical relative of the incense cedar, providing another clue to the land bridge that scientists think may have linked Laurasia and Gondwana until the Early Cretaceous Period.

MAWSONIA

Meaning of name: 'Mawson's animal'
Order: Actinistia
Size, Weight: 55 centimetres long, 4.5 kilos
Location: Africa (Egypt, Morocco, Niger)
Diet: Small fish and water life

Coelacanths evolved nearly 400 million years ago. Among the many kinds alive in dinosaur times was the small coelacanth *Mawsonia*. All coelacanths were thought to have become extinct 65 million years ago until a live one was caught in 1938. Today, coelacanths three times as long as *Mawsonia* live deep in the Indian Ocean near the Comoro Islands.

A living coelacanth

TRIONYX

Meaning of name: 'Three-claw'
Order: Chelonia
Size, Weight: 85 centimetres long, less than 4.5 kilos
Locations: North Africa, Asia and North America
Diet: Plants, fish and insects

This was a common soft-shelled freshwater turtle of the Early Cretaceous. Turtles include terrapins, which live in fresh water, and tortoises, which live on land. One turtle from dinosaur times was the largest turtle ever, with a shell 2 metres in length.

TRIONYX

SARCOSUCHUS

ENRICHING THE WATER

In North Africa 130 million years ago, large plant-eating dinosaurs waded in the swamps. Scientists know from fossils of footprints and dung that these creatures often walked on dry land too. But the sauropods sometimes did live up to the image shown in older dinosaur reconstructions: knee-high or deeper in swampy water, and feeding on the abundant vegetation.

In the tropics today, many large plant-eaters live in and around water. These creatures range from the gentle manatees ('sea-cows') – which graze the rivers, estuaries and coasts of tropical America and West Africa – to African buffalo and the antelope-like lechwe, which are at home in swamps. Many of these animals consume large quantities of fast-growing plants. Otherwise these plants would choke the waterways and crowd out small creatures and slower-growing plants. A large water-loving plant-eater such as a hippopotamus produces enormous amounts of waste. This dung fertilizes the water and nearby soils and is a source of food for fish and other aquatic animals.

An 18-metre-long sauropod dinosaur wades through dense vegetation in the shallow waters of Early Cretaceous North Africa. As this dinosaur moves along the waterways, feeding on the lush plant growth, it leaves behind piles of fresh dung. This waste contains partially digested plant matter that is a feast for water creatures.

In the swamplands, or bayou, of Louisiana in the southern United States, the climate is warm and wet all year round. Wildlife is abundant – wading birds, fish, toads, frogs, turtles and a variety of small mammals. Trees grow tall and close to the edge of the water, which is filled with weeds and other aquatic plants. This environment is like that of Niger 130 million years ago.

Fossil tree trunks from Early Cretaceous Niger have no growth rings within the wood. This suggests that there was little variation in temperature or moisture throughout the year and no single growing season.

In a North African swamp forest 130 million years ago, trees stood on stilt roots **(1)** spread wide to support them in soft mud. Dead branches and fronds fell to the ground and decayed, returning nutrients to the soil. Herbivores ate the plants. Plant-eating dinosaurs lived on land but often fed in the shallow water.

Meat-eaters, from dinosaurs to fish, fed on dead animals **(2)**. Crocodiles **(3)** lay in the water but also basked and hunted on land. Birds **(4)** flew overhead.

Some bony fish in this environment fed only in the shallow waters. Turtles **(5)** moved more widely. They swam in the water and lay in the sun on the shore.

LOST IN THE DESERT

The recent discovery of *Afrovenator* and other dinosaurs in Niger was a combination of good science and good luck. A team of scientists, including Dr Paul Sereno, found dinosaur bones when they were looking for fossil fish in 1990. In 1993, Dr Sereno went back with a larger crew to search for more fossils. He found not only huge plant-eating dinosaurs from 130 million years ago but also the predator *Afrovenator*.

AN AFRICAN ADVENTURE

Afrovenator scavenges on the flesh of a dead sauropod **(1)**. The hungry meat-eater feasts on the muscles of the neck and body cavity. Smaller dinosaurs, turtles, fish and crocodilians also nibble at the remains.

When the scavengers are done, the remaining flesh and skin rot quickly. Rising waters scatter smaller bones. Sediment covers and preserves the biggest bones as fossils.

Dr Sereno was able to tell what *Afrovenator*'s skeleton looked like in real life, even though his crew found only half of its disconnected bones. By comparing the shape and size of the newly found fossil bones with those of other large predatory dinosaurs, he determined that *Afrovenator* looked like a large meat-eater of the Late Jurassic, *Allosaurus*. Missing bones were drawn in by an artist and were sculpted to complete a skeleton.

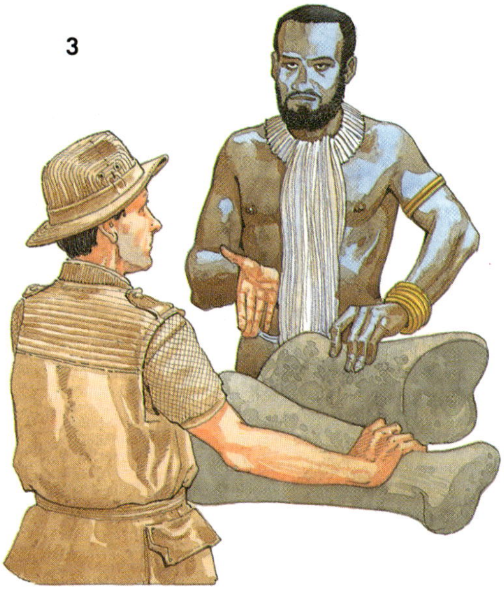

Dr Sereno's team crossed 800 kilometres of the Sahara in Land Rover vehicles to reach the dinosaur graveyards of Niger **(2)**. Stifling daytime heat, bandits, and the lack of roads, signs and accurate maps made the journey difficult. Often the scientists placed boards under the tyres to give them traction when the vehicles got stuck in the sand.

On Dr Sereno's first trip, he and his crew saw a large dinosaur bone in the office of a village leader. Dr Sereno asked the leader **(3)** to take him to the place where the bone was found. In the desert, they found many large dinosaur bones. Many years before, French scientists had found dinosaur fossils nearby but had not excavated them.

Dr Sereno returned to Niger three years later with more researchers. The scientists soon found the dig site and almost at once found their first dinosaur bone **(4)**. It was a 1.5-metre-long upper arm bone of a giant plant-eater. A guide took them to a hilltop, where they found the first fossils of *Afrovenator* – a broken hipbone, leg bones and a claw.

In less than one month of excavation in 1993, Dr Sereno's crew unearthed hundreds of dinosaur bones, including the nearly complete remains of two kinds of dinosaurs new to science – a giant plant-eater and the killer *Afrovenator*. In the first two weeks of exploration they excavated 5 tonnes of fossil bones.

The first few bones of *Afrovenator* that they found were scattered on a hilltop. When the crew began digging, they found vertebrae, hand claws and long skull bones packed with blade-like teeth 5 centimetres in length. Nearby, fossilized pollen, wood from ancient trees, and the bones of sauropod dinosaurs were discovered, giving a good picture of *Afrovenator*'s world. The sauropods' bones were found highly tilted in deep mud, which suggested to the scientists that these big plant-eaters were quickly buried by a flash flood.

Workers uncover the nearly complete fossil skeleton of a giant sauropod in Niger, North Africa, in 1993. The palaeontologists would use a variety of hand tools to unearth the dinosaur remains.

RISE OF THE RAPTORS

CEDAR MOUNTAINS

Utah, North America
125 million years ago

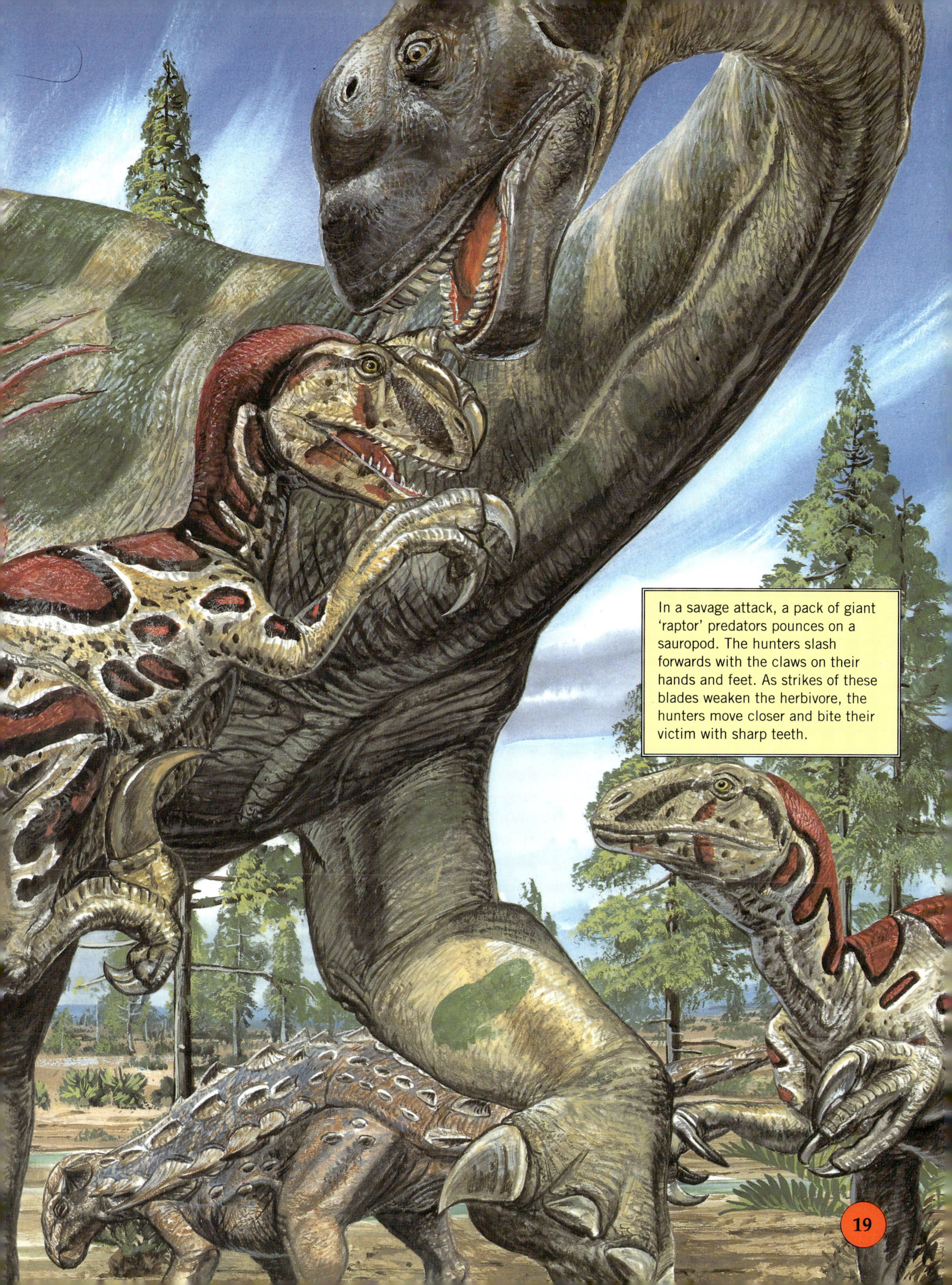

In a savage attack, a pack of giant 'raptor' predators pounces on a sauropod. The hunters slash forwards with the claws on their hands and feet. As strikes of these blades weaken the herbivore, the hunters move closer and bite their victim with sharp teeth.

KILLER CLAWS

New discoveries in Utah reveal a giant breed of the familiar 'raptor' predators. Raptor dinosaurs are named from a Latin word meaning 'robber'. In addition to the sharp, saw-edged teeth of most predatory dinosaurs, these raptors had a curved claw more than 28 centimetres long on each hand and foot.

Utahraptor slashes at the plant-eater 'Gastonia'. Too slow to run from the hunter, the armoured dinosaur crouches, protecting its delicate underbelly as a porcupine does when attacked.

As a raptor dinosaur attacked its prey, it was able to slash with its claws in a slicing arc. The first raptors discovered were small animals from the Late Cretaceous, but new finds in Utah, Japan and Mongolia show that raptors could grow to 6 metres long.

Armoured plant-eaters (from 125 million years ago) are found in Utah. Perhaps the armour of these tank-like creatures helped protect them from the threat of the new 'raptor' hunters. Some sauropods were still living, but they were not so big as those 20 million years earlier. But new large plant-eaters, the iguanodontids (see page 6), were emerging.

Cedar Mountains – Today
Dr James Kirkland visits the site in eastern Utah where a giant-clawed hunter and various plant-eaters were discovered. Sandstones here date from 125 million years ago, when this region was a swampy lowland and warm all year. Now it is a place with hot, dry summers and long, snowy winters.

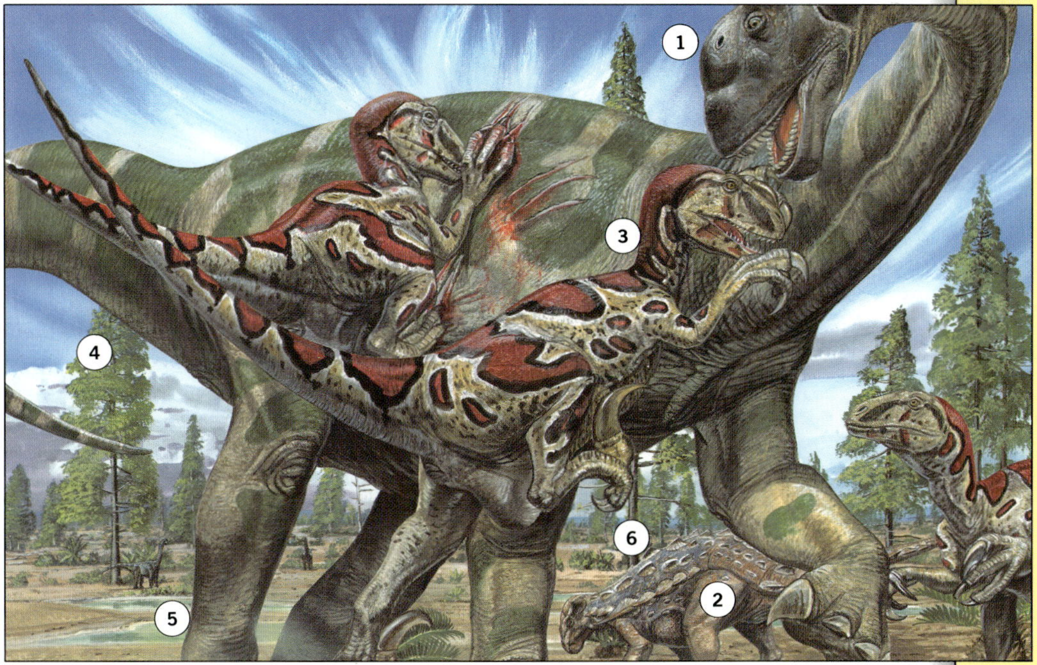

FACT FILE

ANIMALS

1. *Camarasaurus*-like sauropod (KAM-a-ra-SAW-rus)
2. 'Gastonia'-like armoured dinosaur (gas-TOE-nee-a)
3. *Utahraptor* (YOU-ta-RAP-ter)

PLANTS

4. *Brachyphyllum* conifer (BRACK-ee-FILL-um)
5. *Clatophlebis* ferns (KLAT-o-FLEE-bis)
6. Cycads

ALSO AT THIS SITE:
Mormon tea plants

Utah – Then

In this scene in Early Cretaceous North America, both predators and prey are large. A pack of *Utahraptor*, each a tonne in weight, attacks a *Camarasaurus*-like sauropod. Various small predators scavenge on the leftovers of the *Utahraptor* hunt. Other plant-eaters pictured here include an armoured dinosaur related to 'Gastonia'.

Large conifers shade ferns and 60-centimetre-tall cycads in the moist lowland region. In more open areas, bushy Mormon tea plants spread close to shallow pale blue pools of salty water.

Utahraptor was heavily built for a raptor dinosaur, yet it was far less bulky than meat-eaters like *Allosaurus* which preceded it in western North America. Its trim but muscular build suggests to scientists that it could run faster than these earlier predators. *Utahraptor* was probably faster-moving than its prey. These might have included the more heavily built armoured dinosaur 'Gastonia' (see page 23) and *Iguanodon*-like plant-eaters (see pages 6, 32), some of which had sails on their backs.

Utah, Then and Now

Today, the area where *Utahraptor*, the 'Gastonia'-like plant-eater and other creatures lived is a high plateau about 240 kilometres from the Rocky Mountains. During the Early Cretaceous, it was a dry lowland dotted with swamps. The Rocky Mountains had not yet formed.

Globe shows the position of the continents now.

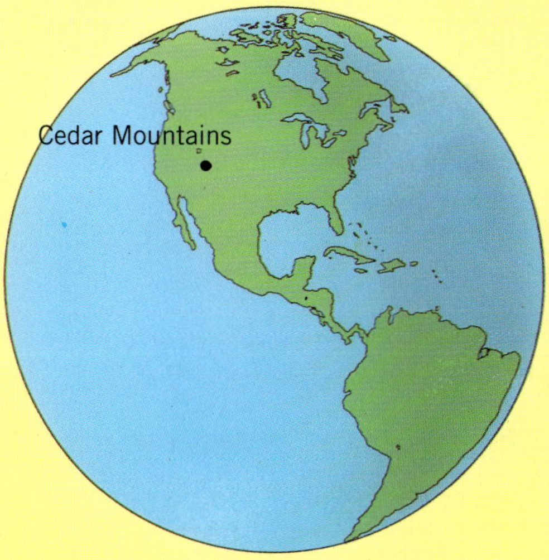

NEW KILLERS UNEARTHED

Raptor dinosaurs, also known as dromaeosaurids, were among the best equipped of meat-eating dinosaurs. Their most terrifying weapons were their enormous sharp toe and hand claws. The recent discovery of *Utahraptor* and other giant raptors from Mongolia and Japan suggests that this line of killer dinosaurs began as large animals in the Early Cretaceous.

***Utahraptor* was far larger** than later raptors, for example *Deinonychus* (western United States, 110 million years ago), *Velociraptor* (Mongolia, 80 million years ago) and *Dromaeosaurus* (North America, 74 million years ago).

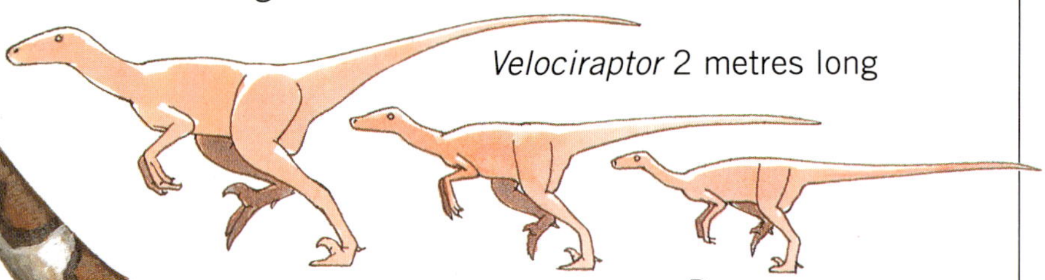

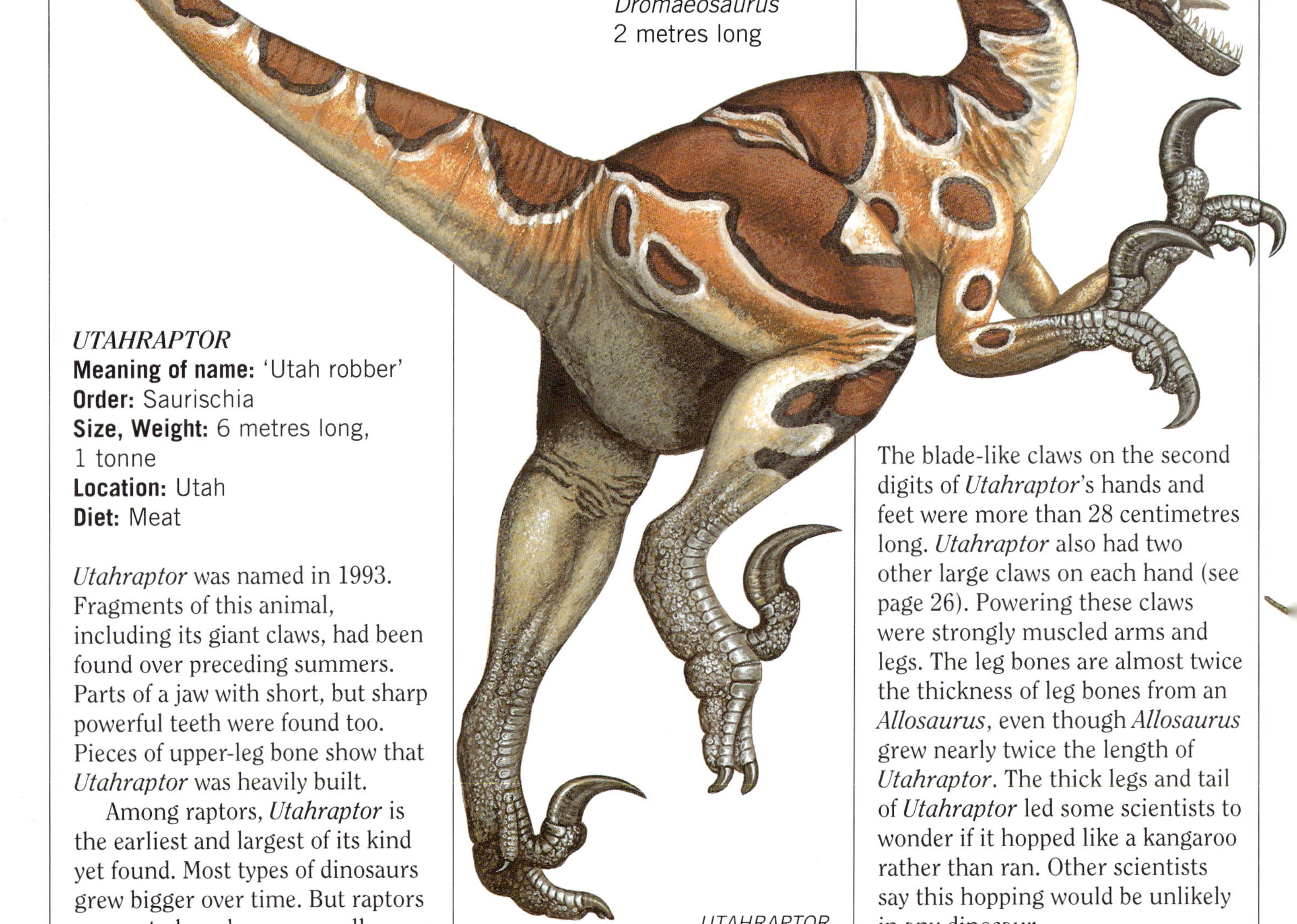

UTAHRAPTOR
Meaning of name: 'Utah robber'
Order: Saurischia
Size, Weight: 6 metres long, 1 tonne
Location: Utah
Diet: Meat

Utahraptor was named in 1993. Fragments of this animal, including its giant claws, had been found over preceding summers. Parts of a jaw with short, but sharp powerful teeth were found too. Pieces of upper-leg bone show that *Utahraptor* was heavily built.

Among raptors, *Utahraptor* is the earliest and largest of its kind yet found. Most types of dinosaurs grew bigger over time. But raptors appear to have become smaller.

UTAHRAPTOR

The blade-like claws on the second digits of *Utahraptor*'s hands and feet were more than 28 centimetres long. *Utahraptor* also had two other large claws on each hand (see page 26). Powering these claws were strongly muscled arms and legs. The leg bones are almost twice the thickness of leg bones from an *Allosaurus*, even though *Allosaurus* grew nearly twice the length of *Utahraptor*. The thick legs and tail of *Utahraptor* led some scientists to wonder if it hopped like a kangaroo rather than ran. Other scientists say this hopping would be unlikely in any dinosaur.

CAMARASAURUS-LIKE SAUROPOD
Order: Saurischia
Size, Weight: 15 metres long, 10 tonnes or more
Location: Utah
Diet: Plants

Parts of two different sauropod dinosaurs have been found near *Utahraptor*. Neither is named yet. They have large spoon-shaped teeth like those of the medium-sized *Camarasaurus* of the Jurassic Period. There are also similarities to *Eucamerotus*, an English sauropod of the Early Cretaceous Period, known for more than a hundred years from fossil fragments. One of the recently discovered sauropods has tailbones linked by ball-and-socket joints, normally seen only in sauropods called titanosaurs.

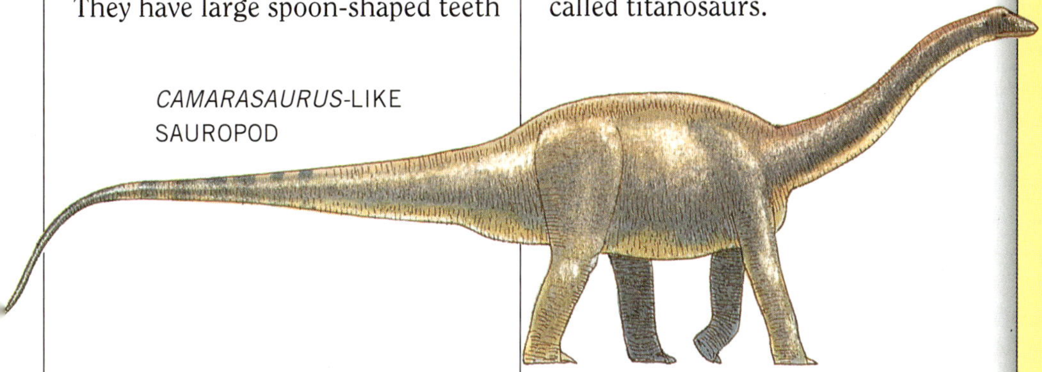
CAMARASAURUS-LIKE SAUROPOD

'GASTONIA'
Meaning of name: 'Gaston's animal'
Order: Ornithischia
Size, Weight: 5.5 metres long, 1 to 2 tonnes
Location: Utah
Diet: Plants

'Gastonia' has yet to be formally named but will likely become an official dinosaur in 1996 or 1997. It is the best known of all the recent discoveries of Early Cretaceous dinosaurs in Utah. Bones from its entire body have been dug up, including protruding spines, several centimetres high, on its neck. It appears to be most closely related to the 4-metre-long armoured nodosaur *Polacanthus* (also known as *Hylaeosaurus*), which lived in England. (Nodosaurs were armoured dinosaurs that lacked a tail club.)

'GASTONIA'

'Gastonia' had thick legs and was built low to the ground. Clearly it was not equipped to run quickly. Plates and spikes covered its entire upper body and this heavy armour might have discouraged most predators.

INSECTS

Insect fossils are not commonly found in these rocks. In Nebraska, in rocks of a similar age, fossil evergreen leaves show tunnels made by caterpillars of primitive moths. Relatives of these moths (Phyllocristinae) are alive today, and their caterpillars feed on sycamore trees.

PLANTS

Forests of tall evergreens grew, as did cycads and bushy Mormon tea plants.

EVERGREEN TREE

SAVANNA WITH SAUROPODS

Though there was no grass in dinosaur times, the open land of Early Cretaceous Utah resembled in many ways the East African savanna of today in the dry season. Tall trees grew by pools and watering holes. Scrubby vegetation grew elsewhere, with ferns, cycads and bushy plants abundant in more open areas. Large animals gathered by the watering holes – both thirsty plant-eaters and carnivores looking for prey.

Utah in the Early Cretaceous was a moister area than it had been in the Late Jurassic. The land was still mostly arid, but now there were more pools and lakes. Turtles, bony fish (including lungfish) and crocodiles inhabited the water. The climate was warm year-round.

Interestingly, many dinosaur types of this time were able to live in a variety of habitats. In Utah, the same animals probably lived in forests and open lands. Animals similar to *Utahraptor* lived in dry environments in Asia. Plant-eaters like those of Utah at the same time lived in a wetter environment in England.

In East Africa today, game animals like these wildebeests spread across the savanna in the rainy season. In the dry season, they move to wetter land or gather around watering holes. About 125 million years ago, dinosaurs in Utah probably migrated in the same way.

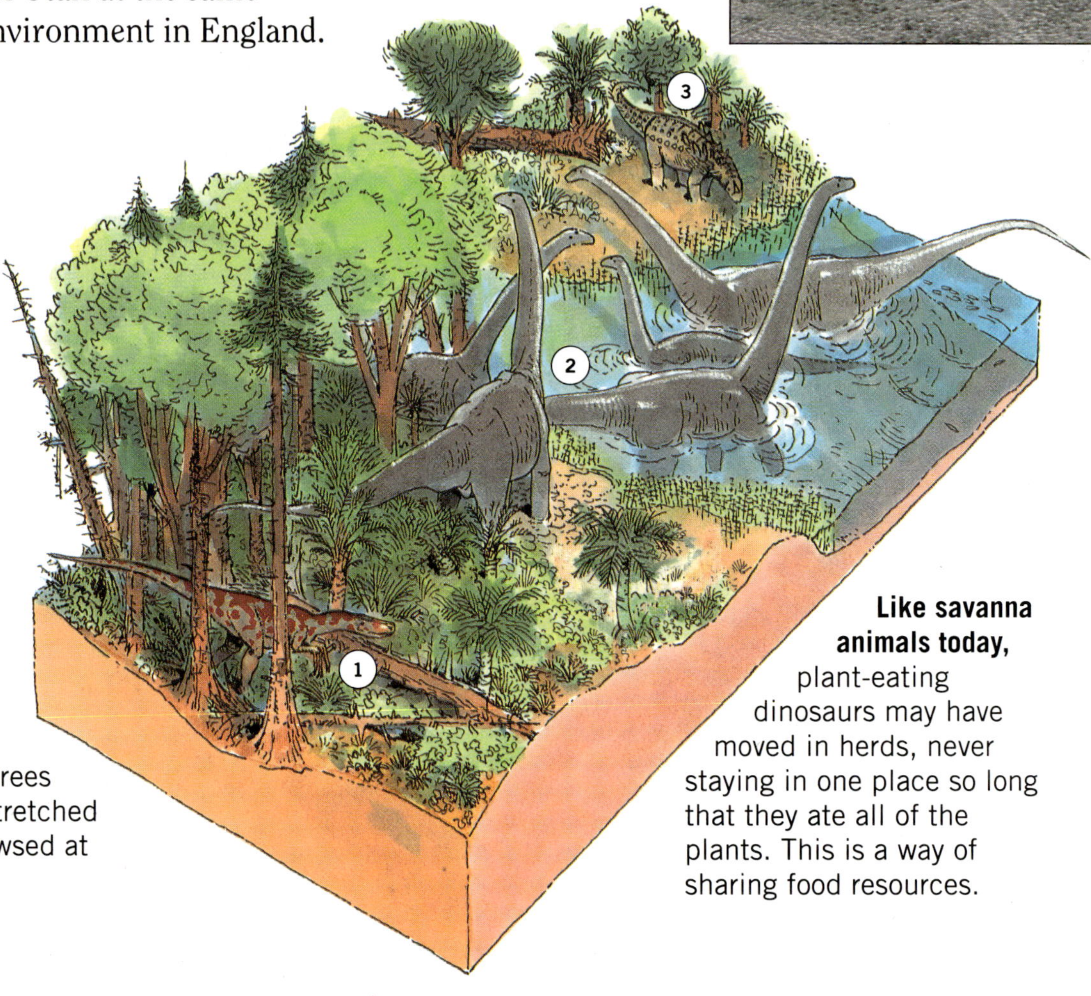

A *Utahraptor* (1) stalks plant-eaters gathered around a pool. The herbivores include sauropods **(2)** and the armoured 'Gastonia' **(3)**. The predator will choose its prey based partly on which plant-eater it prefers to eat and partly on which is the more likely to be an easy kill.

How did so many plant-eaters share one environment? They probably had different feeding niches. Iguanodontids stood on their hind legs to feed from the middle levels of trees (see page 7). Sauropods stretched higher still. 'Gastonia' browsed at ground level.

Like savanna animals today, plant-eating dinosaurs may have moved in herds, never staying in one place so long that they ate all of the plants. This is a way of sharing food resources.

Utahraptor on the run – perhaps chasing a dinosaur prey. The little meat-eaters found in this environment are similar to the small predator *Ornitholestes* from the American West in the Late Jurassic.

Scientists can only guess whether *Utahraptor* ever ran after small predators. It is likely that, unless surprised, little meat-eaters (but not big ones) were too nimble and agile for *Utahraptor*.

How did *Utahraptor* hunt? It might have prowled in packs, as lions do. Using their curved claws, a pack of these 1-tonne monsters would have been able to cut down even the largest sauropods in their world. Or perhaps *Utahraptor* hunted alone? It might have had a camouflage skin colour that allowed it to ambush a passing iguanodontid. It might have leaped on the plant-eater, holding and tearing its victim's flesh with its claws, as a solitary tiger attacks a deer or antelope today.

CLAW CLUE

The claw of *Utahraptor* is one of the most effective killing weapons of any animal. Discovered in 1991, the hand claw of *Utahraptor* was the first clue to the identity of this giant raptor dinosaur. It is similar in shape to claws of the small raptor dinosaurs known for more than fifty years, but it is bigger than any other raptor claw.

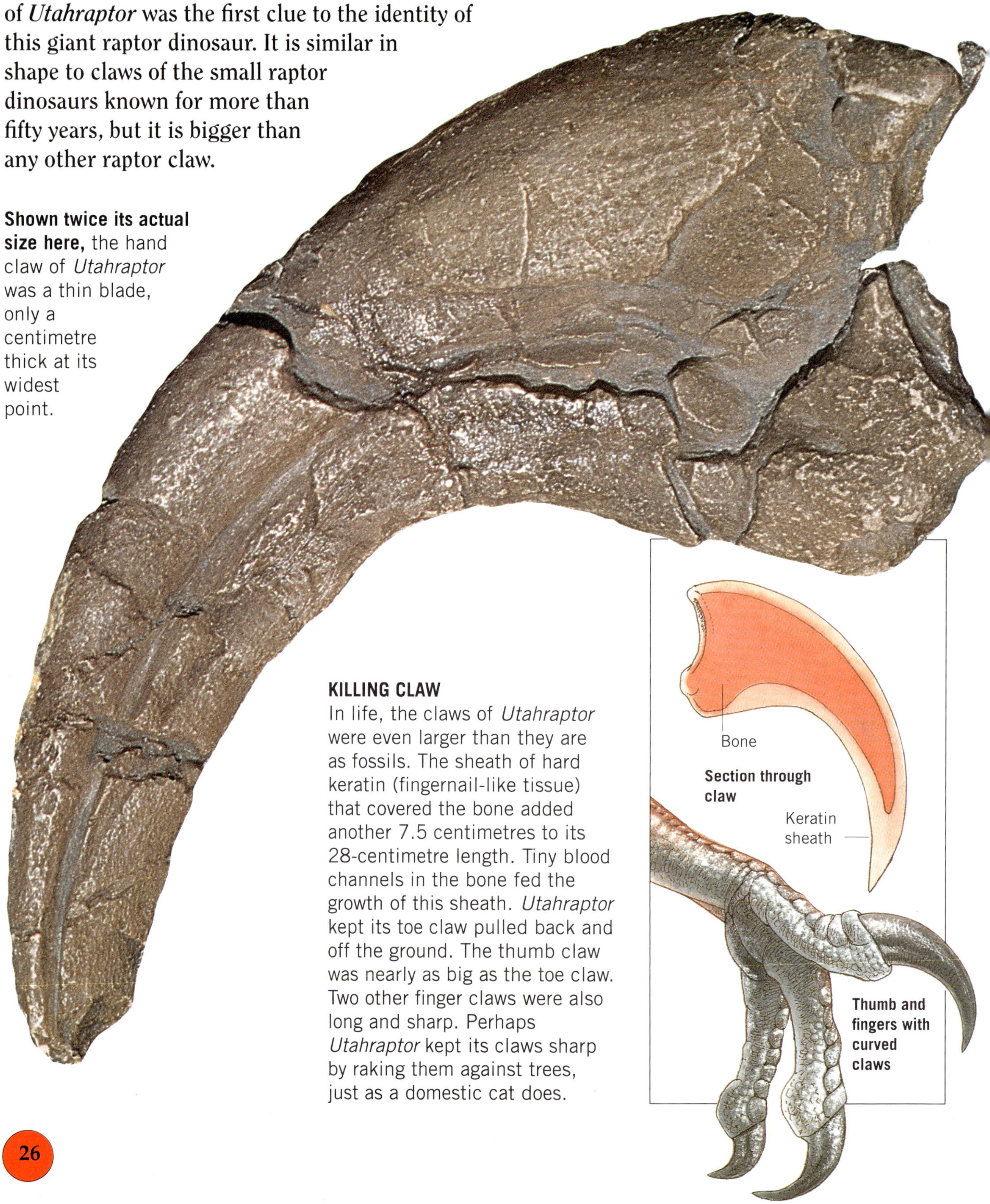

Shown twice its actual size here, the hand claw of *Utahraptor* was a thin blade, only a centimetre thick at its widest point.

KILLING CLAW

In life, the claws of *Utahraptor* were even larger than they are as fossils. The sheath of hard keratin (fingernail-like tissue) that covered the bone added another 7.5 centimetres to its 28-centimetre length. Tiny blood channels in the bone fed the growth of this sheath. *Utahraptor* kept its toe claw pulled back and off the ground. The thumb claw was nearly as big as the toe claw. Two other finger claws were also long and sharp. Perhaps *Utahraptor* kept its claws sharp by raking them against trees, just as a domestic cat does.

Section through claw

Thumb and fingers with curved claws

RAPTOR ATTACK

Utahraptor eyes a 'Gastonia' **(1)**. Before the plant-eater sees that it is being stalked, the *Utahraptor* rushes in towards the slower-moving prey. The armoured dinosaur turns its back towards the *Utahraptor* to protect its vital organs and belly.

Although its claws can slash through hide 2.5 centimetres thick, *Utahraptor* cannot penetrate the thick armour and sharp spikes that cover the back of the plant-eater **(2)**. The raptor's blade-like claws are so narrow that a careless blow might snap one. Frustrated by its lack of success, the predator moves on, leaving the plant-eater unharmed.

The *Utahraptor* is joined by another. Together they overpower a young sauropod **(3)** that they have successfully manoeuvred away from its herd. They slash at the sides and belly of the giant plant-eater, striking with the blades on their toes and hands.

While the weapons of *Utahraptor* are now well known, the way in which it used them is still a mystery. The powerful hind legs of *Utahraptor* were ideal for kicking but not for fast running. Yet most of the large herbivores it might have hunted were not built to move quickly either, and a predator needs only to be faster than its prey to succeed. If fossil footprints are ever found, they could solve the debate about how *Utahraptor* moved. Footprints might also reveal whether *Utahraptor* travelled and hunted alone or in packs.

As with most fossil meat-eaters, there is no direct evidence of *Utahraptor* as a hunter, but its weapons indicate that it was a killer.

Like many predators, *Utahraptor* might have scavenged when possible. This lifestyle saves an animal injury from prey that fight back. Scavenging also uses less energy than hunting does. Most hunts end unsuccessfully for predators of today and the same was probably true in the past.

Utahraptor's habits are not known, but we know something about the lifestyle of its relative *Deinonychus*. In Montana, bones from several *Deinonychus* skeletons have been found among the scattered fossils of the plant-eater *Tenontosaurus*. Scientists think a pack of raptors tore apart the plant-eater, which killed several of the raptors before it died.

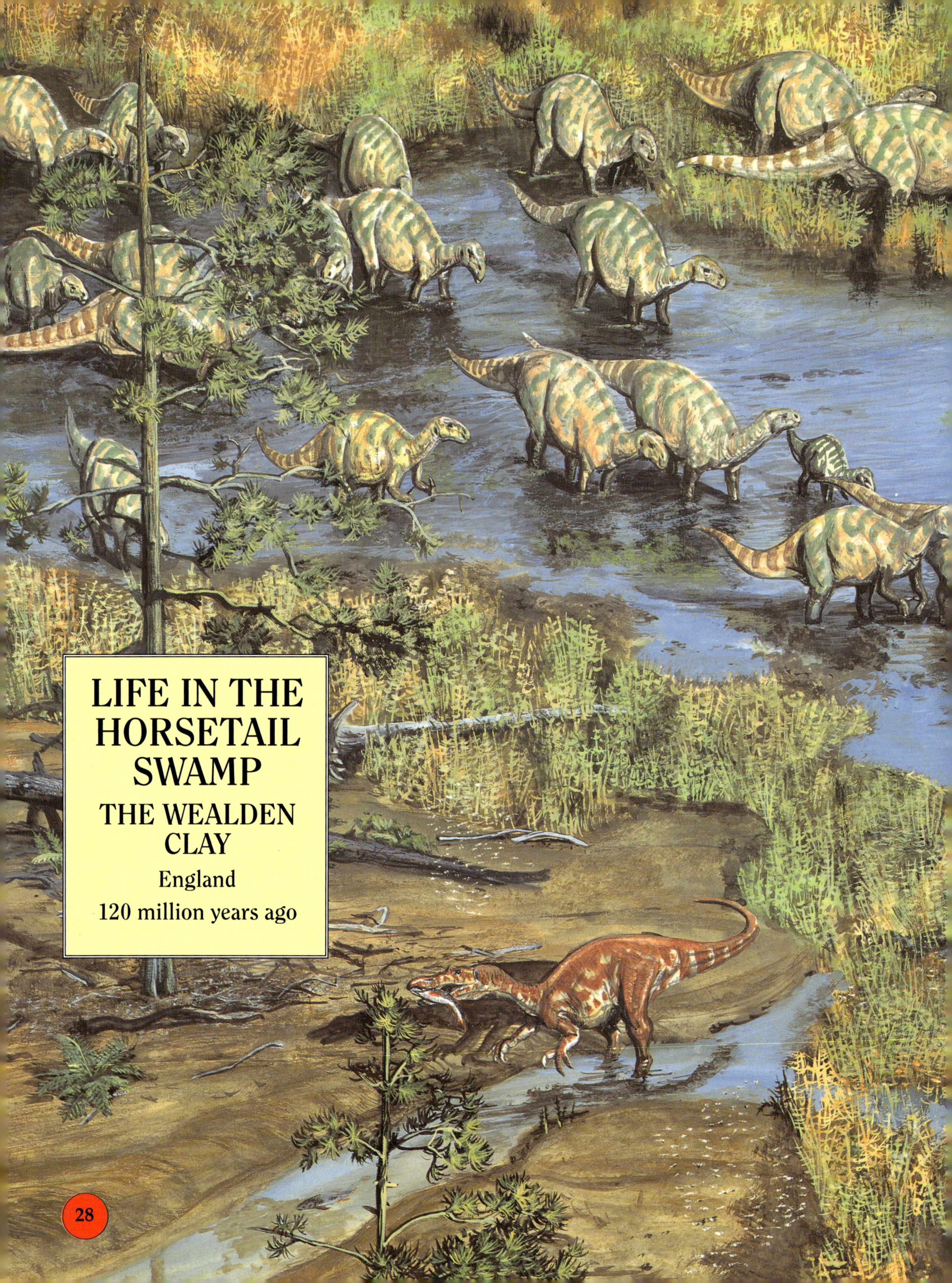

LIFE IN THE HORSETAIL SWAMP

THE WEALDEN CLAY

England

120 million years ago

At the mouth of a river, herds of dinosaurs wade into the shallows to feed on horsetail plants. Nearby, at the water's edge, a large carnivorous dinosaur eats a fish it has caught with its huge sickle-shaped thumb claws. Dragonflies flit overhead.

IGUANODON PARADISE

About 120 million years ago, southern England was a region of lakes and marshes, full of life. The dinosaur *Baryonyx,* with its narrow crocodile-like jaws, caught fish at the water's edge. Other dinosaurs, reptiles and fish were plentiful. The wide variety of plants included some of the first flowering plants.

The Wealden – Today
Southern England now is a cool environment and receives only about 75 centimetres of rain a year. Here, palaeontologists search in the sandstone and clay for more dinosaur fossils from 120 million years ago.

In England 120 million years ago, *Iguanodon* fed on shrubs with little flowers that grew in the marshes and *Baryonyx,* a carnivore, fed on fish (as below).

Flowering plants were greatly outnumbered by more ancient evergreen plants. Ferns flourished in the damp areas. Horsetails, which are large reedy plants, were the most common plants of all. Trees included cone-shaped ancestors of redwoods and the bald cypress trees still seen in warm swamps today. Butterflies, bees and wasps were among the insects that pollinated the early flowering plants.

The plant-eaters of Early Cretaceous southern England include many new kinds of bird-hipped dinosaurs (see page 6). Tiny plant-eaters ran on slim hind legs. Armoured dinosaurs such as *Polacanthus* nibbled at ground-level plants. The most common dinosaur was *Iguanodon* (see pages 6, 32 and 36). This big animal sometimes walked on two legs and other times on all fours. It had more advanced jaws than the sauropods.

The front of its jaw had a wide toothless beak. Nipping off plants with its beak, *Iguanodon* would then mash the plants with the hundred or so teeth in its jaws. The tooth rows were good grinding surfaces. The jaw muscles were strong. When *Iguanodon* brought its jaws together, the upper jaws flexed and slid outside the lower jaws, grinding food between upper and lower teeth. Cheek pouches helped keep food in the mouth. *Iguanodon* had the best chewing mechanism dinosaurs had yet evolved – a big advantage in dealing with tough plant food.

The Wealden – Then A herd of *Iguanodon* grazes on horsetails and other plants in shallow waters where a river meets the sea. *Iguanodon* adults are two different sizes, probably male and female. Other smaller bird-hipped dinosaurs called *Hypsilophodon* also feed on plants. *Baryonyx* dips its claws into the water to snare fish. Horsetail plants grow up to 2 metres high. *Clatophlebis* ferns flourish in the warm, wet conditions. Away from the water, taxodioid trees (related to modern redwoods that live in California) and araucarian conifers grow. Shrub-like flowering plants grow in the clearings. The many kinds of insects include termites, ants, dragonflies, flies and beetles.

FACT FILE

England, Then and Now This area is in Great Britain, which is one of the British Isles. The region now has a cool climate. In the Early Cretaceous, the land was connected to Europe and separated from Greenland and North America by a narrow seaway. The climate was warm and moist, and the land was marshy.

Globe shows the position of the continents now.

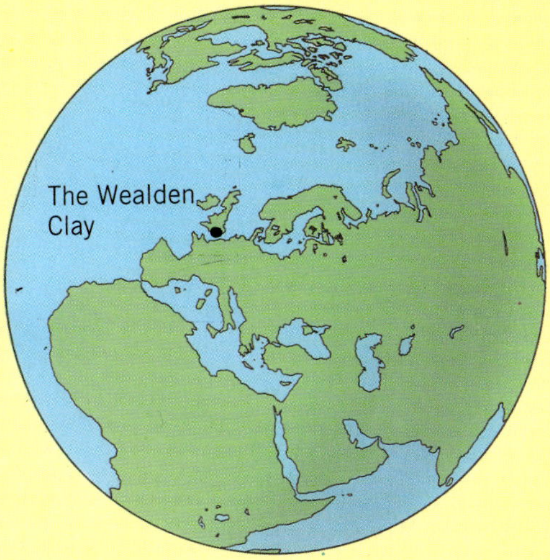

ANIMALS

1. *Baryonyx* (BEAR-ee-ON-icks)
2. Chironomid flies (KY-ro-NO-mid)
3. Dragonfly
4. *Hypsilophodon* (HIP-si-LO-fo-don)
5. *Iguanodon* (ih-GWAN-o-dahn)

PLANTS

6. Araucarian conifer (AR-aw-CARE-ee-un)
7. *Clatophlebis* ferns (CLAY-toe-FLEE-bis)
8. *Equisetum* horsetails (ECK-wee-SEE-tum)

ALSO AT THIS SITE:
Damselflies and weevils
Taxodioid trees (tax-O-dee-oyd)

WORLDWIDE SUCCESS

Iguanodon and other iguanodontids became the common large plant-eaters over much of the world 120 million years ago. Their success was probably due to their sophisticated jaws for chewing plants. With their ability to walk on all fours or rear up on two legs, they might have been able to feed on both the new plants that were appearing and the older types.

***Iguanodon* has been found** in England, Belgium, Germany, Tunisia and the western United States. Related iguanodontids with similar large thumb spikes are known from North Africa, Asia and Australia.

IGUANODON
Meaning of name: 'Iguana tooth' (it has teeth like the modern iguana lizard)
Order: Ornithischia
Size, Weight: 7.5 to 10 metres long, 3 to 7 tonnes
Locations: Western Europe, Tunisia, South Dakota and Utah in the United States
Diet: Plants

Worldwide distribution of iguanodontids, which were kinds of Cretaceous bird-hipped plant-eaters that walked or ran on long hind limbs.

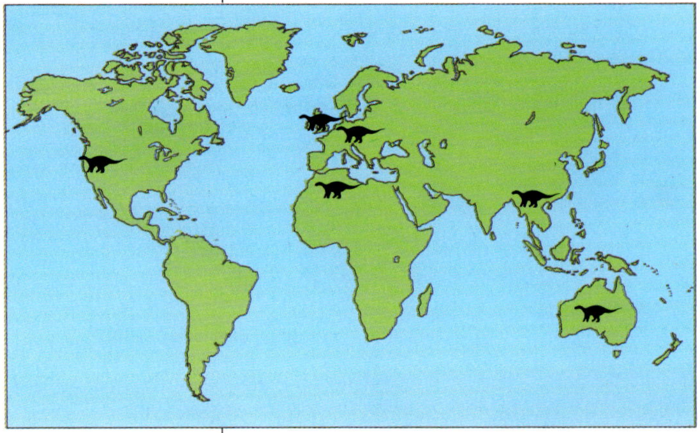

IGUANODON

There are many well-preserved fossils of *Iguanodon*, even a cast of its braincase showing the nerves and blood vessels. *Iguanodon* had a large brain. Its senses were probably good and its behaviour complex.

Adult *Iguanodon* usually walked on all fours. The long straight tail was strengthened by tough overlapping tendons. Young *Iguanodon* had relatively short front legs. They might have walked on two legs more than the adults did. Fossil trackways show several *Iguanodon* heading in the same direction. This suggests that *Iguanodon*, like many plant-eating dinosaurs, were herd animals that migrated regularly.

BARYONYX

BARYONYX
Meaning of name: 'Heavy claw'
Order: Saurischia
Size, Weight: 9 metres long, 1 to 4 tonnes
Location: England
Diet: Fish and other meat

Baryonyx was discovered in 1983, when an amateur fossil collector found its huge claw in a brick quarry in Sussex, England.

Baryonyx's enormous thumb claw was 35 centimetres long in life, curved and pointed at the tip. Its crocodile-like jaws suggest it ate fish. Further evidence includes half-digested fish scales from a 1-metre-long fish found near its rib cage.

Perhaps *Baryonyx* scooped fish from the water with its giant claw, as Alaskan grizzly bears do with their paws. Or it might have snapped up prey with its jaws. Like grizzly bears, *Baryonyx* probably walked on all fours but could stand up straight on its hind legs.

Iguanodon hand

***Iguanodon*'s hands** each had five digits. The three broad middle digits probably had hooves, like a present-day rhinoceros. The wrist bones were fused together for strength. The shorter, slender outer digit (equivalent to our little finger) was flexible. It could bend towards the hand, and might have helped grasp food. The thumb was held off the ground. It bore a sharp spike, which was probably a 'knife' for fighting off attackers (see page 7).

INSECTS

Damselflies and tiny weevils are among the insects preserved in rocks from the English Wealden Formation of 120 million years ago. Weevils are long-snouted beetles that bore into plants. Most weevils today live on and eat flowering plants. But one type, the nemonychid weevils, live in the wood of conifer trees. These weevils were already living inside conifer trees in Early Cretaceous England.

Amber is fossilized resin from conifer trees. This amber, from conifer trees of 120 million years ago, preserved entire damselflies. They are identical to those that lived in Early Cretaceous England and to those seen in some northern conifer forests today.

Damselfly in amber

LAND OF REEDS

Southern England 120 million years ago was a fertile lowland with rivers and streams flowing across the region. When rains were heavy and water levels high, the area was marshy. As the rains ceased, the land became drier and there were many lakes. In time, vegetation filled the lakes and created new land.

For the most part, the ancient Wealden region was warm and moist year-round, much like subtropical marshes today. The river deltas of the Middle East – such as the Tigris-Euphrates Valley, where the first human civilizations dawned thousands of years ago – resemble the marshes of Early Cretaceous England.

In the ancient marshes, *Iguanodon* probably used its spike-thumbed hands to grip the reed-like plants and tear off the edible portions. Many modern plant-eaters are also adapted to live on a limited choice of foods. Koalas, for example, have nimble hands for pulling at the eucalyptus leaves of Australian forests. The giant panda of China is descended from meat-eating bears, but it has evolved grinding teeth and a digestive system for eating only the bamboo plants of its forest habitat.

Marshes become land
Iguanodon feed on weeds **(1)** in a wet lowland. One of the dinosaurs dies at the water's edge as the water level rises in a rainy period. This *Iguanodon*'s body decomposes, leaving only the skeleton **(2)**. Plants grow thickly as water levels drop again. Soon, layers of dead plants cover the bones and prevent more water from entering the lake **(3)**. This section of earth sinks below sea level. Over many millions of years, the marshes become rock and the bones fossilize.

The koala (above) is one of the most specialized animals in Australia. Its diet is almost entirely eucalyptus leaves. Some of these leaves contain poisonous chemicals, but the koala's digestive system renders them harmless.

In the Early Cretaceous Wealden region, fast-growing reeds, cycads, ferns and flowers were excellent food sources for herds of *Iguanodon* and other dinosaurs. *Iguanodon* probably had padded feet that spread their body weight as they waded in the marshes (see page 7). Their grasping hands could hold the swaying marsh plants in order to eat the plants' nutritious and tender new growth. *Iguanodon*'s jaws could process enough plants to provide the energy for an active 3- to 7-tonne animal.

In the midst of a wet lowland, *Iguanodon* graze. They scoop at horsetail reeds, pulling them to their mouths to be cropped off by their wide horny beaks.

Dragonflies hover near the dinosaurs. Beetles, flies and other insects pollinate the flowering plants in the marsh.

FIRST DISCOVERY

Iguanodon and the meat-eater *Megalosaurus* were the first dinosaur fossils found and identified by scientists. *Megalosaurus* lived during the Middle Jurassic Period. The story of *Iguanodon*'s discovery in 1822 by Dr Gideon Algernon Mantell has become legendary. However, scientists today draw a different picture of *Iguanodon* and its life from that suggested by Dr Mantell.

This jumbled partial skeleton of an *Iguanodon* was found in 1834 in a quarry in Kent, England. Dr Mantell's friends bought it for him for a price that was equal to a month's salary for a scientist at that time.

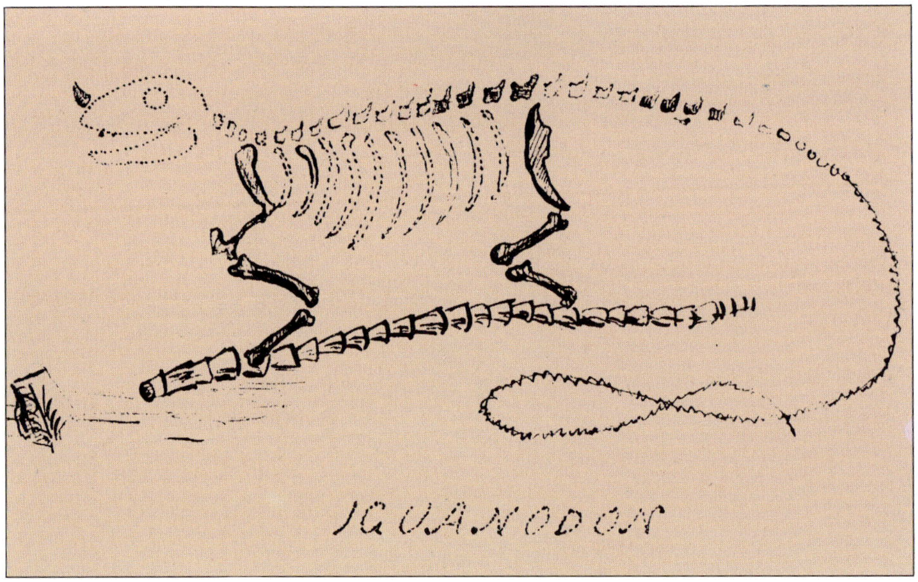

In Dr Mantell's first restoration of *Iguanodon*, he showed the animal as a squat four-legged creature with a horn (really one of its claws) on its snout. He first described *Iguanodon* in 1825 on the basis of the teeth he had found. Dr Mantell believed *Iguanodon* to be a 12-metre-long plant-eating fossil lizard.

At the time, dinosaurs were not known. The term *dinosaur* ('terrible lizard') was not used to describe large extinct reptiles until the year 1842, when the word was invented by British scientist Sir Richard Owen.

Dr Mantell was a family doctor in Sussex, southern England, who collected rocks and fossils. In 1822, he acquired several large mysterious teeth from a nearby rock quarry. Unable to identify them, he showed them to leading scientists in England and France. He believed that the teeth belonged to an extinct creature buried in ancient rock. Scientists doubted the rock's age and thought the teeth belonged to a large fish or mammal.

Dr Mantell felt certain the rocks were very old, but he could not date them accurately. And he was sure that the teeth must belong to an extinct reptile. Comparisons to other teeth suggested to him that these were most like the teeth of the modern iguana lizard, so he called the fossil animal *Iguanodon*, 'iguana tooth'. Some of Dr Mantell's ideas were proved wrong when more discoveries were made, but his ideas were excellent science for their time.

A CHANCE FIND

1

2

An often-told story, in which Dr Mantell's wife, Mary Ann, found the first dinosaur fossil, is now considered a fable. According to this tale, she went with Dr Mantell on a house call in 1822. While he was inside, Mary Ann stayed outside and looked at rocks near the road **(1)**. She saw an object resembling a large tooth **(2)**. Knowing her husband's interest in natural objects for the little museum he had at home, she picked up the tooth and gave it to him. Struck by its unusual appearance, Dr Mantell studied the fossil and concluded that it was the tooth of an extinct reptile.

3

The truth is that quarry workers in nearby Tilgate Forest had found unusual fossils. Dr Mantell dated the rocks at the quarry **(3)** and believed the fossils belonged to an ancient reptile. But only with the find of 1834 (see page 36) was Dr Mantell able to examine more *Iguanodon* fossils **(4)** and create a real picture of the dinosaur.

4

5

In 1855, Waterhouse Hawkins, a British painter and sculptor, created a life-sized *Iguanodon* sculpture for the Crystal Palace Exhibition in London. Just before it was complete, Hawkins and his scientific expert, Sir Richard Owen, held a New Year's Eve dinner inside the mould of the body of *Iguanodon* **(5)**.

Owen commissioned Hawkins to make life-size sculptures of two more dinosaurs for the Crystal Palace Exhibition. They still stand in Sydenham Park in South London. The sculptures were based on only a few fossils, and we now know they were very inaccurate.

DINOSAURS IN THE DARK

DINOSAUR COVE

Australia

110 million years ago

Little dinosaurs with keen eyes find their way along a lakeshore in the daylong twilight of Antarctic early winter. The weather is cool and moist, and a thin layer of ice crackles beneath the feet of the little plant-eaters. Many other animals lurk in the dim light of a long dark season.

DARKNESS DOWN UNDER

In Early Cretaceous times, Australia was much further south than it is today. As a result, the climate was cooler than in present-day Australia. During this warmer era there was no permanent ice, even at the Poles, but Australian dinosaurs and other animals might have sometimes seen snow.

This area offers a glimpse of lifestyles that are far-removed from the usual notions of dinosaur life. The landscape was home to two kinds of small two-legged, sharp-eyed herbivores found nowhere else. Also lurking in the dim light was a small, solidly built predator stalking its prey. Another meat-eating dinosaur darted like an ostrich through the fern underbrush in search of small mammals or hatchling dinosaurs. A large herbivore, a relative of *Iguanodon* with a large bump on its snout, also lived here. A small armoured dinosaur snipped at low-growing plants. (See pages 41, 42–43 and 46.)

The plant-eaters had many food sources to choose from – ferns, cycads, evergreens of many sizes and even a few of the newly evolved flowering plants.

Dinosaur Cove – Today At this site in southeastern Australia, thousands of fragments from dinosaurs of 110 million years ago lie in the sandstone cliffs. The land is dry and cool in winter, hot in summer.

Little *Leaellynasaura* plant-eaters huddle together as a dusting of snow falls. Scientists think Antarctic temperatures in the Early Cretaceous rarely went below freezing, even on the coldest days.

Lush vegetation grows in Early Cretaceous southern Australia. Huge Wollemi pines and araucarian conifers are the tallest trees. Small herbivores eat lower-growing plants, such as ferns, palm-like bennettitaleans and Koonwarra plants (small, scrambling, flowering vines that cover the ground in open places between the trees).

Dinosaur Cove – Then
Small hypsilophodontids (two-legged bird-hipped species) are the most common dinosaurs. Among them are little *Leaellynasaura* and the slightly larger *Atlascopcosaurus*, both of which have large brains and keen eyes to see in the darkness of the polar winter. Bigger still is *Muttaburrasaurus*, a plant-eater similar in body shape and lifestyle to *Iguanodon*. This damp and sometimes cool environment is home to an armoured dinosaur, too. This animal is so recently discovered that scientists have not yet given it a name.

Meat-eating dinosaurs are represented by a stocky predator, no bigger than a person, which was possibly related to *Allosaurus* of Late Jurassic western North America (see page 12). Labyrinthodonts (large amphibians) inhabit the rivers.

Plant life is varied in this moist environment. Ferns and deciduous cycadeoids are among the low-growing plants. In the forest grow huge Wollemi pines, ginkgoes and araucarian trees.

FACT FILE

Australia, Then and Now
Today, Dinosaur Cove is on the southeastern coast of Australia. This part of the continent is about 3,200 kilometres north of the Antarctic Circle. During the Early Cretaceous, Australia was joined to Antarctica, and Dinosaur Cove was with the Antarctic Circle. Although the weather around the world was generally warmer than it is today, the climate in Australia was actually cooler.

Globe shows the position of the continents now.

ANIMALS
1. *Allosaurus*-like theropod (AL-o-SAW-rus)
2. *Leaellynasaura* (lay-EL-in-ah-SAW-ra)
3. *Muttaburrasaurus* (MUT-a-BUR-a-SAW-rus)

PLANTS
4. Araucarian conifer cone (AR-aw-CARE-ee-un)
5. Cycadeoid
6. Ferns
7. Ginkgo
8. Wollemi pine

ALSO AT THIS SITE:
Atlascopcosaurus (AT-las-KOP-ko-SAW-rus)
Labyrinthodonts
Minmi-like ankylosaur (MIN-mee)
Timimus (tim-EYE-mus)

SMALL AND ODD

Australian dinosaurs of 110 million years ago were mostly small compared to those known from elsewhere. They might have been descendants of dinosaurs that were already extinct elsewhere in the world (see page 45). Or, as Australian researchers speculate, they were pioneers – the first of new forms of dinosaurs that would spread across the world.

LEAELLYNASAURA
Meaning of name: 'Leaellyn's lizard'
Order: Ornithischia
Size, Weight: 2 to 3 metres long, 7 to 10 kilos
Location: Australia
Diet: Plants

This little plant-eater was no bigger than a young kangaroo. It was a member of the hypsilophodont family of small, lightly built two-legged herbivores that lived around the world in the Cretaceous. It had a small beak for cutting vegetation.

Fossils of *Leaellynasaura*'s braincase show that it had a big brain compared to its body size, and that it might have been among the smartest of dinosaurs. The area of the brain that controls vision, the optic lobe, was especially large. This suggests that *Leaellynasaura* might have seen particularly well, even in the near-darkness of the polar winters. It had unusual ridges on both sides of its upper teeth.

LEAELLYNASAURA

MINMI-LIKE ANKYLOSAUR
Order: Ornithischia
Size, Weight: Up to 3 metres long, 225 kilos
Location: Australia
Diet: Plants

Fragments of a small ankylosaur found at Dinosaur Cove resemble the fossils of *Minmi*, a small ankylosaur found in later rocks of Early Cretaceous northern Australia. *Minmi* lacked a clubbed tail but, unlike any other dinosaur, under its skin it had armour plates on its belly and alongside its spine. The belly plates were thin and probably not noticeable. The spine plates might have supported the spine or moved the armour on its back and tail.

MINMI-LIKE ANKYLOSAUR

PLANTS

Leaves and pollen fossils from Australia 110 million years ago show some of the plants that lived there at the time. In 1995, scientists in northeastern Australia announced a surprising discovery. They had found living trees previously known only from fossils that are 200 million years old. Named Wollemi pines, the trees are tall, with dense branches of narrow waxy leaves. Their bark is knobby and chocolate-brown in colour. Only a single grove of a few hundred of these trees is known to exist in Queensland, Australia. They would certainly have grown in Early Cretaceous Australia.

WOLLEMI PINE

LABYRINTHODONT

LABYRINTHODONT
Meaning of name: 'Folded tooth'
Order: Temnospondyli
Size, Weight: 3 metres long, 115 kilos
Location: Southeastern Australia
Diet: Small fish, insects, reptiles

Labyrinthodonts were amphibians that were named for their complex teeth. Each tooth was folded in an elaborate pattern. The coelacanth-like lobe-finned fish that were probably their ancestors (see page 10) had very similar teeth.

Until labyrinthodont fossils were found at Dinosaur Cove, these amphibians were thought to have become extinct nearly 200 million years ago. In the dinosaur era, labyrinthodonts were replaced by crocodiles in most of the world. But the waters of Early Cretaceous Australia might have been too cool for crocodiles. Some amphibians today can tolerate colder temperatures than crocodiles can. In the cool waters of the south, the labyrinthodonts might have survived much longer than they did elsewhere because there were no crocodiles to push them out. They are now known to have lived on Earth for 250 million years.

ALLOSAURUS-LIKE THEROPOD
Order: Saurischia
Size, Weight: (Australian form) 3 metres long, 45 to 135 kilos
Locations: Southeastern Australia, North America, Africa
Diet: Meat

Allosaurus is known in western North America as the largest carnivorous dinosaur of the Late Jurassic, growing over 12 metres long. The only fossil found in Australia is a single ankle bone. This bone seems to be from an animal that is smaller than all but three of the fifty-five known specimens of *Allosaurus* from North America. Perhaps *Allosaurus* survived into the Cretaceous in Australia, but in a stunted form. Or the bone may be from a new kind of dinosaur.

ALLOSAURUS-LIKE THEROPOD

APART, FOR ALL TIMES

Millions of years ago in Australia, marsupials (the family of pouched mammals) triumphed over all other mammals. Except for opossums, marsupials became extinct almost everywhere else on Earth. But in Australia, marsupials evolved into a range of successful species, such as the kangaroo and the koala.

A similar process might have been underway among dinosaurs in Australia during the Early Cretaceous. Australia was still linked to Antarctica, but was isolated by valleys and mountains.

Some scientists think that Australia's small allosaurs and ankylosaurs were survivors of animals that had died out in less sheltered places long before. In this same protected Australian environment, an ancient amphibian – a labyrinthodont (see page 43)– survived 90 million years longer than its relatives elsewhere. But fragments of bones from Early Cretaceous Australia suggest to other scientists that advanced kinds of dinosaurs first appeared here at this time. Among these species were dinosaurs with highly developed senses, such as vision.

***Leaellynasaura* and *Atlascopcosaurus* plant-eating dinosaurs** browse in the lush environment of Early Cretaceous southern Australia. They feed on low-growing ferns, cycads and occasional flowering plants. Wollemi pines tower in the background.

Atlascopcosaurus grew to 3 metres long and were named after a drilling company that lent equipment to palaeontologists. *Atlascopcosaurus* was similar to dinosaurs in other parts of the world at this time.

Marsupials, like this kangaroo, keep their babies in pouches. Their young are born at an early stage of development and stay in the mother's pouch until they can fend for themselves. 'Placental' mammals, including humans, give birth to young that have developed more fully inside the mother's womb, or uterus.

One group of early mammals laid eggs and fed their young with milk from specialized glands on the underbelly. Mammals of this type are known as 'monotremes'. Echidnas (spiny ant-eaters) and platypuses are the only living examples of monotremes.

How did Australian dinosaurs cope with the cool of winter? Unlike mammals, they had no fur to warm them and they might not have been warm-blooded. Perhaps they sought shelter in caves or burrows, or they hibernated. They could not have migrated far because of their isolation (see below). Youngsters might have grown fast to adult size, which would have helped them become strong enough to survive.

Separation of Australia and Antarctica due to movements in the Earth's crust.

LABYRINTHODONT

LEFTOVERS OR PIONEERS?
Some Early Cretaceous animals found at Dinosaur Cove, such as the labyrinthodont, are unusually primitive. They died out in other regions 100 million years before; they seem to be 'leftovers' from an earlier age. Dinosaurs like *Leaellynasaura* may have been 'pioneers' – advanced forms compared to the rest of the world. *Leaellynasaura*, with its big brain, might have been an ancestor of the smart dinosaurs that lived elsewhere in the Late Cretaceous.

As Australia separated from Antarctica, dinosaurs might have been isolated in Australia's lush valleys. Did this make the continent a breeding ground for new dinosaur forms? Australian scientists have suggested this idea. Other dinosaur researchers think that this polar land was home to evolutionary leftovers. Island and isolated animals are often stunted in size. A cool climate, as well as geography, might have contributed to the unusual nature of the animals of Early Cretaceous Australia.

TINY TREASURES

Dinosaur fossils from any period are rare in Australia. The country's richest supply of them has been excavated from Dinosaur Cove. There are hundreds of fossil fragments, all of which fit into two museum cabinets. Incomplete as these fossils are, they provide a record of a wide variety of unusual dinosaurs and other animals in Australia.

Prospecting palaeontologists discovered fossils along the granite and sandstone cliffs of southeastern Australia in the early 1980s. Intense digging, drilling and dynamiting of the cliff faces was done over several hot summers.

Leading the excavations were husband-and-wife scientists Thomas Rich and Pat Vickers-Rich. Many volunteers were needed to help haul rocks up from the wave-swept base of the cliffs and then sift through the rocks for fossils. Two caves were dynamited into the cliff face, leaving a column of stone between the caves. The rock richest in fossils proved to be within that column! No complete skeletons were found, but the remains of two kinds of hypsilophodont ('high-ridged toothed') plant-eating dinosaurs and a small meat-eating dinosaur were found.

The Riches named the smaller plant-eating dinosaur *Leaellynasaura* after their daughter, Leaellyn, and the meat-eater *Timimus* after their son, Tim.

The digs at Dinosaur Cove were made along a rough, rocky coast. The palaeontologists used a range of drilling equipment, as here, along with rope pulleys called 'flying foxes' to haul loads of rock to the top of the cliff. After several seasons of intense exploration, the quarries at Dinosaur Cove have been closed. Researchers are now investigating other fossil sites nearby.

LIFE IN THE DARK

Skull bones of *Leaellynasaura* indicate it had a big brain and keen eyes (see page 42). It used its sharp senses to cope with life in the months of gloom and weeks of darkness in ancient polar Australia. Perhaps it used its ability to see in the dark to avoid competitors and predators year-round by doing much of its feeding at twilight and at night.

Embryos of a related dinosaur found in Montana in the United States suggest that a young *Leaellynasaura* was self-sufficient from the time it hatched. Here, a young *Leaellynasaura* hides and rests **(1)**. Meanwhile, one of its parents forages for food in a valley in the dim moonlight **(2)**.

1

The *Leaellynasaura* skull was one of the best fossil finds from Dinosaur Cove. Seen here from above at half its actual size, the skull preserves a cast of the upper surface of the brain. The animal was less than 1.2 metres tall.

The face of *Leaellynasaura* shows its large eyes, and its small beak for cutting vegetation. Here, the dinosaur is pictured with the pupil (the black centre of the eye) wide open to let in as much light as possible for twilight feeding.

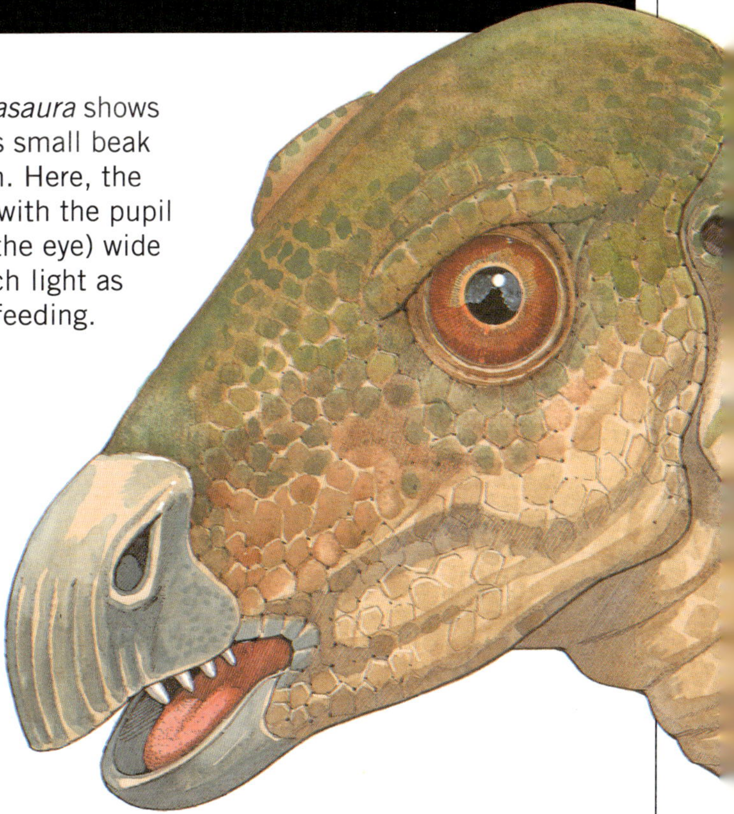

2

The story of Australia's Early Cretaceous dinosaurs is one of strange little creatures in a cool, dark and changing land. During the next and final stage of dinosaur time, the Late Cretaceous, the land and climate continued to change. Dinosaurs became more varied than ever, before they and many other life-forms vanished in a mysterious extinction.

INDEX